Consultative sales: transforming transactions into lasting partnerships

Copyright © 2024 Reginaldo Osnildo
All rights reserved.

PRESENTATION

INTRODUCTION TO CONSULTATIVE SALES

THE CONSULTATIVE MENTALITY

KNOWING YOUR CUSTOMER

BUILDING RELATIONSHIPS OF TRUST

ACTIVE LISTENING

POWERFUL QUESTIONS

CUSTOMIZATION OF SOLUTIONS

NEGOTIATION IN CONSULTATIVE SALES

CUSTOMER RELATIONSHIP MANAGEMENT (CRM)

EDUCATION AND PRODUCT DEMONSTRATION

CONSULTATIVE CLOSURE

FEEDBACK AND FOLLOW-UP

TRAINING AND SKILLS DEVELOPMENT

OVERCOMING OBJECTIONS

MEASURING SUCCESS IN CONSULTATIVE SALES

INTEGRATING SALES AND MARKETING

USE OF TECHNOLOGY IN CONSULTATIVE SALES

DEVELOPING A VALUE PROPOSITION

ACCOUNT MANAGEMENT

TRAINING YOUR SALES TEAM

CULTURAL ADAPTATION

ETHICS AND CONSULTATIVE SALES

EXPANSION AND GROWTH

THE FUTURE OF CONSULTATIVE SALES

REGINALDO OSNILDO

PRESENTATION

Welcome to the world of consultative selling, where every customer interaction is not just a transaction, but an opportunity to build a lasting, trusting partnership. You are about to embark on a journey that will transform the way you sell and, more importantly, the way you relate to your customers. This book is an invitation for you, a sales professional, to update your techniques and strategies to align with the demands of the current, highly competitive and constantly evolving market.

Here, you will find not only a solid theoretical foundation on consultative selling, but also practical strategies that have been shaped and refined to adapt to the new realities of the business world.

This book is the result of in-depth research and practical experience, and was written with a clear purpose: to make knowledge accessible and applicable. You, the reader, are the protagonist of this work. Each chapter was written with the aim of providing you with the tools you need to become not just a salesperson, but a true consultant for your customers. The book not only instructs, but also dialogues with you, encouraging reflection on how these practices can be integrated into your personal sales style and adapted to the unique needs of your customers.

Get ready to explore the next chapter, where we will begin our journey through the universe of consultative sales, defining what they are and how they differ significantly from traditional sales. This knowledge will be the foundation on which we will build all subsequent strategies. Are you ready to transform your sales into strategic and consultative partnerships? So, turn the page and let's get started!

Yours sincerely

Reginaldo Osnildo

INTRODUCTION TO CONSULTATIVE SALES

Consultative selling is much more than simply selling a product or service. This approach transforms traditional sales dynamics by focusing on creating a meaningful relationship between the seller and the customer. Here, you are not just a supplier, but a strategic partner who deeply understands the customer's needs, challenges and objectives. Consultative selling is based on dialogue, adaptation and mutual trust, where value is co-created through collaboration between seller and customer.

The concept of consultative selling emerged as a response to the limitations of transactional sales, which often treat the sales process as a simple exchange of goods for payment. In contrast, consultative selling is characterized by a deeper and more personalized process, which involves understanding and solving real customer problems. The focus is on identifying and meeting the customer's specific needs, often before the customer has even fully recognized them.

HOW CONSULTATIVE SALES DIFFER FROM TRADITIONAL SALES

- **Customer focus** : While traditional selling focuses on the product, consultative selling focuses on the customer. The main objective is to understand the problem that the customer needs to solve and then offer a solution that really meets that need.

- **Long-term relationship** : Consultative selling aims to establish a long-term relationship with the customer, which is beneficial for both parties. This is achieved through an ongoing commitment to customer satisfaction and success, going beyond the simple transaction.

- **Complex sales process** : The consultative sales process is typically more complex and time-consuming than the traditional sales process, as it involves building trust and customizing the offer according to the customer's needs.

- **Education and consultancy** : In consultative sales, you act as a consultant and educator. Part of your job is to educate the customer about how your product or service can solve a specific problem or improve their business.

- **Value creation** : The consultative approach focuses on creating value for the client, which often results in more expensive but more effective and beneficial solutions in the long term. This contrasts with traditional sales, where the focus may be more on price and less on added value.

By adopting consultative selling, you not only increase your chances of sales success, but you also increase customers' perception of the value of your offer. This results in higher customer satisfaction and loyalty rates, as well as a stronger competitive position in the market.

By understanding what consultative selling is and how it differs from traditional selling, you are more prepared to embrace this powerful approach. Now that you understand the fundamentals, you're ready to explore how to develop the right mindset to be effective in consultative selling. In the next chapter, we'll dive into the consultative mindset, a crucial component for transforming the way you sell and building lasting relationships with your customers.

Get ready to open your mind and deepen your understanding in the next chapter, where we explore the nuances of the consultative mindset and how it can be cultivated to transform your sales interactions into valuable consultancies. Let's go on this journey together?

THE CONSULTATIVE MENTALITY

Adopting a consultative mindset is essential for any professional who wants to excel in consultative selling. This mentality goes beyond simple sales techniques; it encompasses a philosophical approach that puts the customer at the center of all decisions. Let's explore how you can develop this mindset and why it's crucial to success in consultative selling.

WHAT IS CONSULTATIVE MENTALITY?

The consultative mindset is a way of thinking that emphasizes deep understanding of customer needs, empathy, ethics, and collaboration. It requires you, as a salesperson, to see yourself as a consultant who helps the customer solve problems, not just someone who sells products or services. This approach requires a willingness to invest time and effort to understand and resolve customer pain points, and to build a trusting relationship that transcends the immediate transaction.

CHARACTERISTICS OF CONSULTATIVE MENTALITY

- **Empathy**: Put yourself in the customer's shoes to truly understand their needs and challenges.

- **Active listening**: Listen carefully and engagedly, capturing not only the words, but also the context and emotions behind them.

- **Focus on solutions**: Thinking about how to solve problems, instead of just selling a product. This involves a detailed analysis of customer needs and customizing solutions that meet those needs effectively.

- **Integrity and transparency**: Being honest about what your solution can and cannot do for the customer, building a relationship based on trust.

- **Patience and perseverance**: Understand that some sales processes can be long and that it is necessary to maintain focus on the long-term relationship with the customer.

WHY IS CONSULTATIVE MENTALITY IMPORTANT?

Adopting a consultative mindset allows you to differentiate yourself in a competitive market. In a world where many products and services are viewed as commodities, the ability to provide value through a consultative approach is a significant competitive advantage. Additionally, this mindset fosters customer loyalty and increases the chances of renewals and business recommendations, as customers tend to connect more with brands and individuals who show a true interest in helping them achieve their goals.

Developing a consultative mindset is an ongoing process that requires dedication, reflection, and practice. By strengthening this mindset, you will be able to connect with your customers in a more meaningful way, creating not just sales, but lasting partnerships based on mutual respect and effective collaboration.

Are you ready to apply this mindset and learn more about your customers in a deep and effective way? In the next chapter, we'll explore how knowing your customer can transform the way you conduct sales. Together, we will discover techniques for understanding your client's needs and challenges, providing the basis for a truly consultative and strategic partnership. Shall we continue our journey?

KNOWING YOUR CUSTOMER

At the heart of consultative selling is the ability to deeply understand who your customers are. This chapter will guide you through the process of getting to know not just the superficial facts about your customers, but also their deeper motivations, their challenges, and how they perceive the world. Learning to decipher these elements is crucial to transforming simple transactions into lasting strategic partnerships.

WHY KNOWING YOUR CUSTOMER IS CRUCIAL?

- **Customization** : The more you know about your customers, the more able you are to adapt your solutions to their specific needs. This not only increases the effectiveness of your solution, but also demonstrates to the customer that you genuinely value their business.

- **Anticipating needs** : Understanding your customer allows you to anticipate problems or needs that they themselves may not have realized yet. This establishes you as a proactive partner, someone who brings solutions before problems even become evident.

- **Building trust** : When customers see that you truly understand their needs and challenges, they are more likely to trust you. Trust is the foundation of any long-term relationship and is especially important in consultative selling.

- **Continuous improvement** : By knowing your customers well, you can continue to improve and adjust your offerings to better serve them over time, which can lead to repeat business and referrals.

HOW TO DEEPLY KNOW YOUR CUSTOMER

- **Research** : Before meeting with a client, do your homework. This includes researching not just the company, but also the industry they operate in and the specific challenges they face.

- **Active listening** : During customer interactions, practice active listening. This means paying attention not only to what is said, but also to what is left out, and to nonverbal cues.

- **Ask deep questions** : In addition to standard questions, ask questions that encourage the customer to think and reveal more about their true challenges and needs.

- **Continuous feedback** : Establish a process for regular feedback, allowing you to adjust your approaches and solutions based on what works best for the customer.

- **Use CRM efficiently** : Customer Relationship Management (CRM) systems are vital tools for maintaining detailed information about customer interactions, preferences and purchasing history, which can be used to personalize future interactions.

Knowing your customer is not a task you complete once and mark as done; it is an ongoing process that deepens as the relationship grows. By taking the time to truly understand your customers, you position yourself as an essential advisor to them, not just a salesperson.

Ready to further deepen your ability to build solid, trusting relationships? In the next chapter, we'll explore strategies for building and maintaining trusting relationships with customers, essential for consultative selling. Continue your journey with us and transform your sales approach into a true strategic partnership. Shall we move forward?

BUILDING RELATIONSHIPS OF TRUST

Trust is the backbone of consultative selling. This chapter is dedicated to exploring how you can build and sustain trusting relationships, transforming sales interactions into lasting, beneficial partnerships. Here, you will learn practical strategies that you can apply immediately to start strengthening your bonds with customers.

THE IMPORTANCE OF TRUST IN CONSULTATIVE SALES

Building trust is not just good sales practice; It is essential for long-term survival and growth in today's business environment. Trust-based relationships:

- **They facilitate open and honest negotiations**, which can lead to better agreements for both parties.

- **Encourage customer loyalty**, resulting in repeat business and less price sensitivity.

- **Increase the likelihood of recommendations**, as satisfied and confident customers are more likely to recommend your services to others.

HOW TO BUILD TRUSTING RELATIONSHIPS

- **Consistency and predictability**: Show your customers that they can count on you to be consistent and reliable. Deliver what you promise and always be available to support them.

- **Honesty and transparency**: Be transparent about the benefits and limitations of your products or services. Honest communication is crucial to establishing and maintaining trust.

- **Empathy and understanding**: Demonstrate empathy and make a genuine effort to understand the customer's concerns and needs. Show that you care not just about the sale, but about the customer's success and well-being.

- **Proactivity**: Anticipate customer needs and offer solutions before they ask for them. This shows that you are attentive and committed to the partnership.

- **Respect for the client's time and resources** : Value your clients' time as much as you value yours. Be efficient in your communications and meetings, and ensure that each interaction adds value to them.

- **Regular feedback** : Establish an ongoing dialogue with your customers for feedback. Use this information to continually improve the service you offer, demonstrating that you value their opinion and are committed to adapting your solutions to their evolving needs.

Trusting relationships are not built overnight. They require patience, dedication and an ongoing commitment to excellence and integrity in all interactions. By adopting the strategies presented in this chapter, you will be well equipped to develop and maintain relationships that not only stand the test of time but are also mutually beneficial and satisfying.

Ready to take your consultative selling skills to the next level? In the next chapter, we'll dive into active listening techniques, an essential skill for any consultative salesperson who wants to truly understand and meet their customers' needs. Continue with us on this journey and discover how to further improve your ability to build lasting partnerships. Let's go together in this?

ACTIVE LISTENING

Active listening is one of the most crucial skills in consultative selling. This chapter will guide you through effective techniques for improving your active listening skills, ensuring that you understand not only what your customer says, but also what they really mean and need. Active listening allows you to identify opportunities to deepen the relationship and customize your solutions more effectively.

WHAT IS ACTIVE LISTENING?

Active listening is the process of listening with full attention, understanding the speaker's message, and responding in a way that promotes mutual understanding. It is not limited to listening to the words spoken, but involves interpreting the context, feelings and underlying needs.

WHY IS ACTIVE LISTENING IMPORTANT IN CONSULTATIVE SALES?

- **Deep understanding** : Helps you understand not only the customer's explicit needs, but also their unexpressed concerns and motivations.

- **Relationship building** : Shows the customer that you value their opinions and genuinely care about meeting their needs, strengthening the relationship.

- **Identification of opportunities** : Allows you to identify opportunities to offer additional solutions that the customer may not have initially considered.

- **Problem solving** : Facilitates the identification and resolution of problems effectively, which can improve customer satisfaction and loyalty.

TECHNIQUES TO IMPROVE ACTIVE LISTENING

- **Maintain full focus on the customer** : During conversations, avoid distractions. Focus fully on what the customer is saying without planning your response as they speak.

- **Use positive body language** : Show interest and openness through your body language. Nod your head, maintain eye contact, and adopt an open, receptive posture.

- **Reflect and clarify** : Periodically reflect on what was said to ensure you understood correctly. Use phrases like "If I understand correctly, you are saying that..." to confirm your understanding.

- **Ask pertinent questions** : Ask questions that deepen your understanding of the customer's needs and desires. Open-ended questions are especially useful for encouraging the customer to talk more about their concerns.

- **Avoid interrupting** : Allow the client to speak without interruptions. Showing patience can encourage you to share more detailed and important information.

- **Summarize and confirm** : At the end of the conversation, summarize the main points and confirm next steps to ensure both sides are aligned.

Improving your active listening skills is a fundamental step towards becoming an effective sales consultant. By implementing these techniques, you will be better equipped to understand your customers' true needs, build stronger relationships, and provide solutions that truly make a difference.

Ready to take your consultative selling skills even deeper? In the next chapter, we'll explore the power of powerful questions to uncover real customer needs and further strengthen your consultative selling skills. Let's move forward on this path together?

POWERFUL QUESTIONS

Mastering the art of asking powerful questions is essential for any salesperson who aspires to transform simple transactions into deep consultative partnerships. This chapter focuses on how you can use strategic questions to go beyond superficial answers, allowing you to uncover your customers' true needs and wants. Let's explore techniques that will help open up new possibilities and strengthen your sales relationships.

THE VALUE OF POWERFUL QUESTIONS

Powerful questions are those that provoke thought, encourage reflection, and lead clients to consider their situations in a new light. They are essential because:

- **Reveal valuable information** : Well-formulated questions can unearth needs and problems that not even the customer had fully identified.

- **Strengthen relationships** : By showing genuine interest in customers' concerns and aspirations, you strengthen trust and loyalty.

- **Facilitate solution customization** : Deeply understanding what the customer really needs allows you to customize your solutions more effectively.

- **Establish you as a consultant** : Powerful questions demonstrate your competence and your commitment to offering not just products, but true and adapted solutions.

POWERFUL QUESTION TYPES

- **Open-ended questions** : These questions facilitate more detailed answers and are crucial for starting an in-depth dialogue. Examples include "What do you think is stopping your business from reaching its full potential?" or "How do you imagine the ideal solution to this problem?"

- **Exploration questions** : Use these questions to delve deeper into a specific point or to explore the customer's emotions and motivations. For example, "Can you give me an example of when this was a problem?" or "How does this affect your team?"

- **Reflective questions** : These questions encourage the client to think and reflect on their current and future situation. Questions like "What would happen if you didn't do anything about this problem?" or "Where do you see your business in five years?"

- **Confirmation questions** : These are used to ensure that you correctly understand the customer's situation or need. "So, if I understand correctly, you are looking for a solution that can do X and Y, correct?"

STRATEGIES FOR ASKING POWERFUL QUESTIONS

- **Do your homework** : The more you know about the client and their business before a meeting, the more specific and impactful your questions can be.

- **Actively listen** : Use what you learned in the previous chapter to really listen to the customer's responses, which can give you insights into what questions to ask next.

- **Stay curious** : Cultivate an attitude of genuine curiosity. Be genuinely interested in the customer's responses, without rushing to sell your product.

- **Adapt to the flow of the conversation** : Be prepared to change your questions based on the direction the conversation is going. Flexibility can lead to important discoveries.

Powerful questions are a crucial tool in any consultative salesperson's arsenal. They open doors and create the foundation for relationships of trust and collaboration. By honing your ability to ask strategic questions, you will position yourself as an indispensable advisor to your clients.

Are you ready to customize solutions that meet your customers' exact needs? In the next chapter, we'll explore how you can effectively customize solutions, ensuring your offerings are as unique as the challenges your customers face. Shall we continue on this journey of transformation?

CUSTOMIZATION OF SOLUTIONS

The ability to customize solutions that meet your customers' exact needs is one of the hallmarks of consultative selling. In this chapter, we'll explore how you can develop custom solutions that not only solve customer problems but also add significant value to your business. Customization goes beyond simply adapting products; it is a holistic approach that considers all aspects of the client's situation.

THE IMPORTANCE OF CUSTOMIZATION IN CONSULTATIVE SALES

- **Competitive differentiation** : In a saturated market, the ability to offer customized solutions can differentiate your company from the competition.

- **Increased customer satisfaction** : Solutions that precisely meet customer needs tend to result in greater satisfaction and loyalty.

- **Better customer outcomes** : Customized solutions are more effective because they are designed specifically to solve the customer's unique problems.

- **Long-term relationships** : By demonstrating a commitment to the customer's specific need, you strengthen the relationship and encourage ongoing commitment.

STRATEGIES TO CUSTOMIZE SOLUTIONS

- **Deeply understand customer needs** : Use the active listening techniques and powerful questions discussed in previous chapters to gain a deep understanding of customer challenges.

- **Involve the customer in the development process** : Make the customer a partner in the solution creation process. This not only ensures the solution is relevant and personalized, but also increases customer engagement and satisfaction.

- **Use appropriate technology and tools** : Employ technologies that allow flexibility and customization in solutions. CRM and data analysis tools can offer valuable insights that help customize solutions.

- **Continuous feedback and adjustments** : Customization does not end with the delivery of the solution. Keep an open line of communication for feedback and be ready to make adjustments as needed.

Customizing solutions requires creativity, empathy and an ongoing commitment to excellence in customer service. By taking the time to understand and meet each customer's specific needs, you not only improve the effectiveness of your solutions, but also strengthen your company's position as a thought leader and trusted partner.

Ready to explore the techniques needed to negotiate these customized solutions? In the next chapter, we will discuss advanced negotiation strategies in consultative sales, essential to ensuring that both sides of the table win. Let's continue together on this transformative journey?

NEGOTIATION IN CONSULTATIVE SALES

Negotiation is a critical component in consultative selling, not just as a means of closing deals, but as a way of cementing relationships and ensuring that both sides realize significant and sustainable value. This chapter will cover essential negotiation strategies that can be used to ensure that your customized solutions are not only accepted, but also valued by the customer, reinforcing partnership and mutual trust.

FUNDAMENTALS OF CONSULTATIVE NEGOTIATION

Negotiation in consultative sales differs significantly from the traditional style of negotiation because it focuses less on winning the argument and more on finding a solution that benefits both parties. Here are the fundamentals that guide consultative trading:

- **Focus on win-win solutions** : Look for agreements that offer clear benefits for both sides, strengthening the relationship in the long term.

- **Transparency** : Maintain open communication about the capabilities and limitations of proposed solutions.

- **Flexibility** : Be prepared to adapt your offering as customer needs and feedback evolve.

- **Active listening** : Use your active listening skills to understand the customer's concerns and priorities and negotiate accordingly.

EFFECTIVE NEGOTIATION STRATEGIES IN CONSULTATIVE SALES

- **Preparation** : Before entering into a negotiation, be well prepared with all the information about the customer and their needs, as well as the details of your offer.

- **Building Value** : Emphasize how your solution meets or exceeds customer needs in ways that other solutions cannot . Use data, testimonials and case studies to reinforce your argument.

- **Use of strategic concessions** : Determine in advance what concessions you can make that are low cost to you but high value to the customer.

- **Setting expectations** : Be clear about what you can offer and be prepared to explain how your solution may require compromises or adaptations.

- **Collaborative closing** : Involving the client in the closing process can help ensure that all parties are aligned and satisfied with the proposed agreement.

Negotiating effectively in a consultative sales context requires a mix of preparation, empathy, and customer-focused strategy. By implementing these techniques, you will not only be able to close more sales, but also strengthen the customer-seller relationship, transforming negotiations into opportunities to deepen the partnership.

Ready to take customer relationship management to a new level? In the next chapter, we'll explore how to use CRM tools to support your consultative selling strategies while maintaining a focus on personalization and customer satisfaction. Follow us to discover how to effectively integrate technology and relationships into your consultative sales.

CUSTOMER RELATIONSHIP MANAGEMENT (CRM)

Customer Relationship Management (CRM) technology is a crucial ally in consultative sales. This chapter will cover how to effectively use CRM tools to maximize your sales, personalize communication, and maintain a quality relationship with your customers. Let's explore best practices and strategies for integrating CRM into the consultative sales process.

THE ROLE OF CRM IN CONSULTATIVE SALES

CRM is not just a tool for organizing contact information; is an integral system that can manage and analyze customer interactions throughout the entire relationship lifecycle. Here are the main benefits of using CRM in consultative sales:

- **Centralization of information** : Keeps all customer information in one accessible place, making it easier to monitor and personalize interactions.

- **Data analytics** : Provides valuable insights into purchasing patterns, customer preferences and interaction history, allowing you to personalize your offers.

- **Improved communication** : Helps ensure all customer communications are consistent and relevant, improving overall sales effectiveness.

HOW TO USE CRM TO IMPROVE CONSULTATIVE SALES

- **Customer segmentation** : Use CRM to segment customers based on criteria such as industry, size, purchasing behavior, and specific needs. This segmentation allows you to create more personalized offers that are more likely to meet customer expectations.

- **Interaction Record** : Document all customer interactions in the CRM system. This includes calls, emails, meetings and feedback, ensuring you don't miss important details and can deliver a more considered and personalized service.

- **Task automation** : Automate recurring tasks such as

follow-ups and sending thank you or informative emails. This helps maintain efficiency and allows you to focus on more strategic aspects of consultative selling.

- **Analysis and reporting** : Use CRM's analysis features to evaluate the effectiveness of your sales strategies and make adjustments as necessary. Detailed reports can help identify trends, measure customer satisfaction, and optimize sales processes.

- **Integration with other tools** : Integrate your CRM with other tools such as marketing platforms, data analysis tools, and financial management software. This integration can provide a more complete view of the customer and improve coordination between different departments.

Investing in a robust CRM tool and knowing how to use it effectively can significantly transform your consultative sales approach. By facilitating personalization, communication and data management, CRM not only improves efficiency but also helps you build stronger, longer-lasting customer relationships.

Ready to further deepen your knowledge in consultative sales? In the next chapter, we'll explore how to effectively educate your customers about your products or services, an essential component of making the purchasing decision easier and strengthening trust in the relationship. Continue with us on this transformative journey!

EDUCATION AND PRODUCT DEMONSTRATION

Customer education is a key part of consultative selling. This chapter explores how you can use product or service education as a strategic tool to build trust and support the customer decision process. By educating your customers, you not only inform, but also add value by demonstrating the real potential of your solutions to meet their specific needs.

THE IMPORTANCE OF CUSTOMER EDUCATION IN CONSULTATIVE SALES

Educating the customer goes beyond simply presenting product features and benefits. It involves:

- **Communicate value** : Show how the product or service can solve a problem or improve a process in the customer's business.

- **Develop trust** : By providing clear, actionable information, you establish your company as a trusted resource and an invested partner in customer success.

- **Facilitate purchasing decisions** : Well-informed customers are better able to make purchasing decisions that are aligned with their business needs and objectives.

STRATEGIES TO EFFECTIVELY EDUCATE YOUR CUSTOMERS

- **Personalize customer education** : Tailor your educational content to your customer's specific needs. Use data collected through your CRM to customize presentations and materials in ways that resonate with specific customer problems and challenges.

- **Utilize different formats** : Combine multiple content formats, such as videos, webinars, handouts, and live demos, to suit different learning styles and increase customer engagement.

- **Hands-on demonstrations** : Whenever possible, offer hands-on product demonstrations, which allow the customer to see how the solution works in a real or simulated environment. This can be particularly effective in overcoming objections and reinforcing the value of the product.

- **Education workshops** : Host workshops or training sessions that not only introduce the product but also teach something of value that the customer can apply regardless of purchase.

- **Support materials** : Provide detailed support materials that customers can take with them. These materials must be easy to understand and rich in useful information that reinforces the message and value of your solution.

- **Ongoing feedback** : After educational sessions, collect feedback to understand how you can improve future sessions and what information was most valuable to customers.

Customer education is essential to success in consultative selling. By investing time to educate your customers about your products and services, you not only increase transparency and trust, but you also establish a solid foundation for lasting relationships and strategic partnerships. With well-informed customers, the chances of long-term satisfaction and loyalty increase significantly.

Ready to move forward? In the next chapter, we'll cover consultative closing techniques that ensure customer satisfaction and encourage long-term relationships. Let's continue this journey to transform your sales into true consultative partnerships.

CONSULTATIVE CLOSURE

Consultative closing is a crucial aspect of consultative selling, where the focus is not just completing a sale, but ensuring that the close brings lasting benefits to both sides. This chapter will explore effective strategies for closing sales in a way that reinforces trust and fosters the continuity of the business relationship.

THE IMPORTANCE OF A CONSULTATIVE CLOSURE

Consultative closing differs significantly from traditional closing because it seeks to create a positive shopping experience and a foundation for future interactions. That includes:

- **Customer validation** : Ensure that all customer doubts are clarified and that they feel confident in their purchasing decision.

- **Respect for the client's decision-making process** : Recognize that each client may have a different decision-making process and adapt the closing approach to those specific needs.

- **Promotion of lasting relationships** : View each sale closing as a step towards an ongoing relationship, not as an end.

EFFECTIVE STRATEGIES FOR CONSULTATIVE CLOSING

- **Benefits summary** : Reiterate the benefits of your solution, emphasizing how they meet the specific needs previously discussed with the customer. This helps reinforce the relevance of the solution and the customer's decision.

- **Flexible terms** : Offer flexible terms when possible, such as adjustable payment terms or personalized packages, which can make the purchasing decision easier for the customer.

- **Use closing questions** : Use questions that prompt action, such as "Do you think this solution could improve the efficiency of your process?" or "Would you like to start on this project next week?"

- **Risk minimization** : Reduce the risks perceived by the customer by offering guarantees or trial periods. This can increase customer confidence in their purchasing decision.

- **Soft confirmation** : Instead of pushing for a hard close, use a soft confirmation that allows the customer to feel like they are choosing to proceed, such as "How would you like to proceed if you decide this is the right solution for you?"

Consultative closing is an art that balances persuasion with sensitivity to the client's needs. By implementing these strategies, you will not only increase the chances of successfully completing sales, but you will also lay the foundation for a lasting partnership based on mutual respect and ongoing satisfaction.

Are you ready to go the extra mile and continue to build that valuable relationship? In the next chapter, we will explore the importance of feedback and follow-up after the sale, essential for maintaining and deepening the relationship with the customer. Stay with us to learn how these elements are fundamental in consultative selling.

FEEDBACK AND FOLLOW-UP

After closing a sale, a consultative salesperson's work is far from over. Feedback and continuous monitoring are essential to maintaining and strengthening customer relationships, ensuring not only continued satisfaction, but also opening doors to future business opportunities. This chapter explores how to implement an effective feedback system and follow-up strategies that benefit both you and your customers.

WHY ARE FEEDBACK AND FOLLOW-UP CRUCIAL?

- **Satisfaction guarantee** : Monitoring helps to ensure that the customer is satisfied with the solution purchased and that it meets the expectations created during the sales process.

- **Identification of new needs** : Maintaining regular contact allows you to identify new needs that may arise as the client's business evolves.

- **Fostering customer loyalty** : Customers who feel that their suppliers are genuinely interested in their success tend to be more loyal and likely to do repeat business.

EFFECTIVE STRATEGIES FOR FEEDBACK AND FOLLOW-UP

- **Establish a follow-up plan** : Set a schedule for regular post-sales contact, which could include calls, visits, emails or virtual meetings, depending on the customer's preference.

- **Implement satisfaction surveys** : Use survey tools to collect feedback on customer satisfaction with the product or service and the sales process. This not only provides valuable data but also shows the customer that you value their opinion.

- **Offer proactive support** : Don't wait for the customer to report a problem. Offer proactive support, checking to see if everything is going well and if there is anything you can do to help.

- **Use CRM for monitoring** : Keep records of all interactions in the CRM system. This will help personalize follow-up, ensuring that no important information is missed and that each interaction is relevant and useful.

- **Create opportunities for Upsell and Cross-Sell** : Based on customer feedback and emerging needs, identify opportunities to offer additional products or services that can benefit the customer.

PRACTICAL EXAMPLE

Suppose you sell software systems. After implementation, you can schedule a series of training sessions and periodic reviews to ensure the customer is using the software effectively. During these sessions, you may discover additional needs that can be met with upgrades or new modules, providing more value to the customer and generating new sales.

Feedback and follow-up are fundamental components of consultative selling, transforming each sale into a starting point for a lasting relationship. By implementing these strategies, you will not only increase customer satisfaction but also lay a solid foundation for future business opportunities.

Ready to further deepen your consultative selling skills? In the next chapter, we will discuss how to identify and develop the skills needed to be effective in consultative selling. Stay with us on this journey of continued growth and long-term success.

TRAINING AND SKILLS DEVELOPMENT

To be successful in consultative selling, it's not enough to just understand the product or service you offer; It is crucial to possess and hone a set of skills that allow you to effectively interact with customers and deeply understand their needs. This chapter focuses on how to identify and develop these essential skills, ensuring you are equipped to perform high-level consultative selling.

CRUCIAL SKILLS IN CONSULTATIVE SALES

- **Active listening** : As previously explored, the ability to listen actively is fundamental to truly understanding customers' needs and desires.

- **Empathy** : The ability to put yourself in the customer's shoes, understanding their challenges and concerns, not only on a business level, but also on a personal level.

- **Effective communication** : The ability to clearly communicate your ideas and value solutions in a way that resonates with the customer.

- **Problem solving** : The ability to think creatively when solving problems, offering solutions that effectively meet the specific needs of the customer.

- **Negotiation** : Skills to negotiate not only contract terms, but also to manage expectations and find solutions that benefit all parties involved.

- **Relationship management** : Ability to develop and maintain strong, long-term relationships with customers.

STRATEGIES TO DEVELOP THESE SKILLS

- **Formal training** : Investing in professional training courses can be an excellent way to develop specific consultative sales skills.

- **Mentoring and coaching** : Working with a mentor or coach who has experience in consultative selling can provide valuable learning and personalized guidance.

- **Regular practice** : Since many sales skills are honed with experience, looking for opportunities to practice these skills in real-world situations is crucial.

- **Continuous feedback** : Requesting feedback regularly, both from customers, colleagues and superiors, can help identify areas for improvement and confirm strengths.

- **Self-assessment and reflection** : Regularly taking time to reflect on your customer interactions and sales success can help you understand what works well and what can be improved.

EXAMPLE DEVELOPMENT PLAN

Suppose you want to improve your negotiation skills. You could:

- Participate in a workshop specializing in negotiation techniques.

- Practice negotiation scenarios with colleagues or a coach.

- Request specific feedback after each real trading session.

- Study successful cases in negotiation to understand different strategies and styles.

Developing effective consultative selling skills is an ongoing process that requires dedication and commitment. By identifying skills in need of development and implementing strategies to improve them, you will position yourself as a highly competent and trustworthy consultative sales professional.

Ready to see how these skills translate into practical success? By focusing on understanding the customer's challenges and proposing personalized and effective solutions, the consultative salesperson establishes himself as an indispensable partner in the customer's success.

Ready to overcome objections and continue to expand your consultative selling skills? In the next chapter, we'll explore effective strategies for handling and overcoming objections during the consultative sales process. Continue your learning journey with us!

OVERCOMING OBJECTIONS

Overcoming objections is a natural and inevitable part of the consultative sales process. This chapter focuses on how you can effectively identify, understand, and respond to customer objections, turning potential barriers into opportunities to deepen the business relationship and solidify trust.

UNDERSTANDING THE OBJECTIONS

Objections arise for a variety of reasons, often as an expression of concern or uncertainty on the part of the client regarding the proposal offered. They may be related to cost, product suitability, uncertainty about ROI (return on investment), or even resistance to change. Understanding the nature and origin of the objection is crucial to being able to respond to it effectively.

STRATEGIES TO OVERCOME OBJECTIONS

- **Active listening** : Before responding to an objection, it is essential to ensure that you truly understand the customer's concern. Active listening also demonstrates respect and consideration for the customer's feelings and opinions.

- **Validate the customer's concern** : Acknowledge and validate the customer's objection. This doesn't mean agreeing, but showing that you understand where they are coming from and that their concerns are important to you.

- **Respond with information** : Many objections can be overcome by providing additional information that the customer may not have. This could include data on the product's effectiveness, testimonials from other customers, or relevant case studies.

- **Rephrase the objection** : Often, an objection reveals an opportunity to rephrase the proposal in a way that better aligns with the client's needs and desires. This may involve highlighting different aspects of the product or service that may not have been initially evident.

- **Offer a demo or trial** : If possible, offer a demo or trial period so the customer can see for themselves how the product or service can solve their problem.

- **Create a sense of urgency** : If the objection is related to hesitation in making an immediate decision, you can help create a sense of urgency by highlighting the cost of not acting or the immediate benefits that may be lost.

PRACTICAL EXAMPLE

Suppose a customer objects to the cost of a piece of software you are selling, arguing that it is too expensive. You can respond by highlighting how software can increase efficiency, reduce long-term operating costs, and offer a return on investment that would make the initial cost seem insignificant. Additionally, you could offer flexible payment options or highlight specific features that offer additional value that other competing products don't have.

Overcoming objections is an essential skill in consultative selling and requires practice, patience and a deep understanding of the customer's needs and concerns. By addressing objections strategically, you not only increase the chance of closing a sale, but also strengthen the relationship of trust with the customer.

Ready to explore how to measure the success and impact of your consultative sales strategies? In the next chapter, we will discuss effective methods for evaluating and optimizing your consultative sales practices. Keep improving your skills with us!

MEASURING SUCCESS IN CONSULTATIVE SALES

Evaluating success in consultative sales goes beyond simply calculating sales and revenue. This chapter explores how you can measure the impact and effectiveness of your consultative sales strategies, using metrics that reflect both sales performance and the depth and health of customer relationships.

IMPORTANCE OF MEASUREMENT OF SUCCESS

Measuring success in consultative selling is essential for:

- **Evaluate the effectiveness of strategies** : Determine which tactics are working and which need adjustments.

- **Justify the investment** : Demonstrate the return on investment (ROI) of your sales activities to internal stakeholders.

- **Continuously improve performance** : Use data-driven insights to refine sales approaches and techniques.

METRICS TO MEASURE SUCCESS IN CONSULTATIVE SALES

- **Sales conversion rate** : Measures the effectiveness of converting prospects into paying customers, which can indicate the effectiveness of your closing techniques and the quality of your initial interactions.

- **Customer Lifetime Value Value - CLV)** : Evaluates the total value that a customer brings to the company over time. A high CLV suggests that the sales strategy is creating lasting, profitable relationships.

- **Customer satisfaction** : Measured through satisfaction surveys, NPS (Net Promoter Score), or direct feedback, this indicator reflects how well customer needs are being met.

- **Customer retention rate** : Indicates the percentage of customers who remain with the company after the first deal. High retention rates are a sign of strong, satisfying customer relationships.

- **Customer Acquisition Cost (CAC)** : Calculates the total cost involved in acquiring new customers. In consultative sales, a higher CAC may be justified by the more personalized approach and the potential for higher CLV.

- **Average time to close** : Measures how long it takes, on average, to close a deal after the first contact with a prospect. This can help assess the efficiency of sales processes and the impact of different negotiation techniques.

STRATEGIES TO IMPROVE SUCCESS METRICS

- **Continuous improvement** : Use data and feedback to identify areas for continuous improvement, adjusting strategies and processes as necessary.

- **Training and development** : Invest in ongoing training for your sales team to ensure everyone is equipped with the skills needed to execute effective consultative selling.

- **Relationship focus** : Prioritize developing long-term relationships, not just short-term sales. This may involve deepening knowledge about customer needs and customizing solutions.

Measuring success in consultative selling requires a multifaceted approach that considers both financial metrics and indicators of customer satisfaction and loyalty. By understanding and applying these metrics, you can not only justify the value of consultative selling, but also continue to refine your strategies for even better results.

Ready to further integrate your sales strategies with your marketing strategies? In the next chapter, we'll explore how to align consultative sales with marketing strategies to maximize results and drive growth. Continue your journey to becoming a consultative sales expert!

INTEGRATING SALES AND MARKETING

Effective integration between sales and marketing teams is crucial to the success of consultative selling. This chapter will discuss how you can align these two functions to create a coherent approach that expands the reach of your initiatives and maximizes market impact.

THE IMPORTANCE OF SALES AND MARKETING INTEGRATION

Collaboration between sales and marketing allows:

- **Consistent messages** : Ensures that all communications with the market are aligned, reinforcing the company's brand and value proposition.

- **Generation of qualified leads** : Marketing can use sales insights to create campaigns that attract leads more aligned with the ideal customer profile.

- **Resource optimization** : Avoids duplication of efforts and ensures that both departments are working with the same objectives and metrics.

STRATEGIES TO ALIGN SALES AND MARKETING

- **Setting shared goals** : Establish clear goals that both departments can understand and be co-responsible for, such as number of qualified leads, conversion rate and revenue growth.

- **Regular communication** : Hold regular cross-team meetings to discuss progress, share customer insights, and adjust strategies as needed.

- **Personalized content** : Use the information collected by the sales team about customers' needs and pain points to create marketing content that speaks directly to potential buyers' points of interest.

- **Use of integrated technology** : Adopt CRM and marketing automation tools that allow you to easily share information between teams, helping to track customer engagement and campaign effectiveness.

- **Cross-training** : Encourage training that allows members of each team to better understand the roles and challenges of the other side, promoting greater empathy and collaboration.

PRACTICAL EXAMPLE

Suppose a software company is launching a new product. Marketing creates a campaign focused on the product's technical features, while the sales team finds that customers are more interested in how the product can save time and reduce costs. By aligning these insights, marketing can adjust the campaign to highlight economic benefits, while sales uses technical materials at specific moments in the sales cycle.

Integrating sales and marketing strategies in a consultative approach not only increases the effectiveness of both functions, but also improves customer experience and operational efficiency. By working together, sales and marketing can drive sustainable growth and build a solid competitive advantage.

Ready to explore how technology can further improve the consultative sales process? In the next chapter, we'll look at how to use emerging technologies to enhance your sales approach and achieve exceptional results. Stay with us to discover tools that can transform your consultative sales strategies.

USE OF TECHNOLOGY IN CONSULTATIVE SALES

Technology plays a crucial role in modernizing consultative sales, enabling greater efficiency, better communication and deeper analysis. This chapter covers how you can integrate advanced technologies into your consultative sales strategy to improve each step of the sales process, from prospecting to closing and post-sales.

BENEFITS OF TECHNOLOGY IN CONSULTATIVE SALES

- **Automating repetitive tasks** : Automating tasks like data entry and email tracking frees up time for salespeople to focus on higher-value activities like developing customer relationships.

- **Access to real-time data** : Tools such as CRM and data analytics provide valuable insights into customer behavior, sales trends and campaign performance, helping you make data-driven decisions.

- **Improved communication** : Communication and collaboration platforms improve interaction both internally between teams and with customers, facilitating a more fluid and transparent exchange of information.

- **Personalization at scale** : Artificial intelligence and machine learning technologies enable the personalization of offers for individual customers on a previously impractical scale.

IMPACT TECHNOLOGIES IN CONSULTATIVE SALES

- **CRM (Customer Relationship Management)** : CRM tools are essential for managing interactions with customers, storing important information and accessing interaction histories that can be crucial during negotiations.

- **Artificial intelligence (AI)** : AI can be used to analyze large volumes of customer data and generate insights that help predict customer needs and personalize the sales approach.

- **Marketing automation** : This technology helps you create and manage marketing campaigns that nurture leads over time, delivering personalized content based on customer interactions and behavior.

- **Data analytics platforms** : Analytics tools help you better understand customer purchasing patterns, effectiveness of sales strategies, and areas for improvement.

- **Communication and collaboration tools** : Solutions such as Slack, Microsoft Teams and Zoom facilitate fast and effective communication, essential for coordination in consultative sales.

IMPLEMENTING TECHNOLOGY EFFECTIVELY

- **Choose appropriate tools** : Assess your team's specific needs and choose tools that align with your strategic goals.

- **Training and adoption** : Ensure your team is trained to use new technologies efficiently. Resistance to change is common, and proper training can help mitigate this challenge.

- **Continuous analysis** : Use data collected through these technologies to continually review and adjust your strategies, ensuring you are meeting customer expectations and achieving your sales objectives.

Integrating technology into the consultative sales process not only increases efficiency, but also enriches the customer experience and offers new opportunities for personalization and engagement. By adopting and adapting these technologies, you can significantly expand your ability to deliver solutions that meet the complex needs of modern customers.

Ready to explore even more about how to develop a clear and compelling value proposition? In the next chapter, we will discuss how to develop and communicate your value proposition to stand out in the competitive market. Continue on this journey to strengthen your consultative selling skills!

DEVELOPING A VALUE PROPOSITION

The value proposition is fundamental in consultative sales, as it defines why a customer should choose your company over others. This chapter explores how you can develop and articulate a value proposition that resonates deeply with your customers, setting your solutions apart in the competitive marketplace.

THE IMPORTANCE OF A STRONG VALUE PROPOSITION

An effective value proposition:

- **Differentiates your offer** : Clarifies how your product or service differentiates itself from the competition.

- **Focuses on customer needs** : Focuses on how you can solve specific problems or improve the customer's situation.

- **Increases the relevance of your solution** : Helps the customer understand why your solution is the best option for their needs.

STEPS TO DEVELOP AN EFFECTIVE VALUE PROPOSITION

- **Understand your customer** : Get to know your customers' needs, challenges and desires in depth. Use this information to create a proposal that speaks directly to their most critical pain points.

- **Identify your differentiators** : Determine what makes your offer unique in the market. This may include superior quality, exceptional customer service, innovative technology, or more competitive pricing.

- **Communicate clear benefits** : Instead of focusing on product features, highlight the benefits these features bring to the customer.

- **Use simple and direct language** : Avoid jargon and technical terms that could confuse or alienate customers. Your value proposition should be easy to understand and remember.

- **Test and refine** : Present your value proposition to a small group of customers or colleagues to get feedback. Use this information to make necessary adjustments.

EXAMPLE OF VALUE PROPOSITION

Suppose you are selling an advanced CRM system. Instead of simply highlighting features like marketing automation and third-party integrations, your value proposition could be: "Our CRM simplifies your customer relationship management, allowing you to automate repetitive tasks and focus on closing more sales, increasing revenue by up to 30% in one year."

COMMUNICATING YOUR VALUE PROPOSITION

Once developed, the value proposition must be communicated consistently across all customer touchpoints, including:

- **Website** : Integrate the value proposition into your homepage, product pages, and company bio.

- **Marketing materials** : Ensure all marketing materials such as brochures and advertisements clearly reflect your value proposition.

- **Sales pitch** : Equip your sales team with a clear pitch that highlights your value proposition during customer interactions.

Developing a clear and compelling value proposition is essential for standing out in a competitive market and for effectively communicating the value your company brings to your customers. This proposal not only guides your marketing and sales strategies, but also serves as a constant reminder of your commitment to meeting customer needs.

Ready for the next step? In the next chapter, we'll explore best practices for managing accounts to maximize customer retention and satisfaction. Continue improving your consultative sales techniques to reach and exceed your goals.

ACCOUNT MANAGEMENT

Effectively managing customer accounts is vital in consultative selling as it not only helps maintain customer satisfaction and loyalty, but also maximizes opportunities for repeat sales and upselling . This chapter explores account management best practices that strengthen customer relationships and ensure continued satisfaction.

THE IMPORTANCE OF EFFECTIVE ACCOUNT MANAGEMENT

Effective account management allows you to:

- **Deeply understand customer needs** : Keeps you informed about changing customer needs and expectations, enabling proactive adjustments to the solutions offered.

- **Anticipate problems** : Helps identify and resolve potential problems before they negatively affect the relationship.

- **Maximize customer value** : Ensures that the customer is making the most of the products or services offered, maximizing their return on investment.

STRATEGIES FOR ACCOUNT MANAGEMENT

- **Customer segmentation** : Classify your customers based on various criteria, such as sales volume, growth potential, or complexity of needs. This allows you to customize strategies for different customer groups.

- **Development of account plans** : Create an account plan for each important customer, detailing strategies for maintaining and expanding these accounts. Include specific objectives, planned initiatives, and timelines for review.

- **Regular and personalized communication** : Maintain open lines of communication with your customers. Send regular updates about new products, services, or company changes that might affect them.

- **CRM Usage** : Employ CRM systems to monitor interactions, manage contact information, and analyze sales data to better understand customer trends and behaviors.

- **Offering additional value** : Constantly look for ways to add value to the relationship, whether through expert advice, additional training or access to exclusive resources.

TECHNIQUES TO IMPROVE CUSTOMER RETENTION

- **Periodic account reviews** : Conduct regular account reviews to discuss challenges, successes and areas for improvement. Use these meetings to reaffirm the value your company provides.

- **Loyalty and rewards programs** : Consider implementing programs that reward customers for their loyalty and continued business.

- **Feedback and action** : Consistently solicit feedback from customers and, most importantly, act on that feedback to improve your services.

- **Account team enablement** : Ensure all team members deeply understand customers' products, services and markets. Invest in regular training to keep your team updated and effective.

Competent account management is essential to success in consultative selling, creating a solid foundation for long-lasting, profitable relationships. By implementing these strategies, you not only improve customer satisfaction and retention, but also position your company as a valuable and reliable partner.

In the next chapter, we'll explore how to train your sales team to adopt and implement consultative selling practices. Stay with us to discover how to empower your team to maximize their performance and contribute significantly to the company's success.

TRAINING YOUR SALES TEAM

Success in consultative sales depends not only on the strategies and tools used, but crucially on the people who implement them. This chapter covers how you can train your sales team to adopt and implement consultative selling practices, ensuring everyone is aligned and empowered to maximize their performance.

THE IMPORTANCE OF TRAINING IN CONSULTATIVE SALES

Proper training provides several benefits:

- **Improves competence and confidence** : Empowers salespeople with the skills and knowledge needed to face complex sales challenges.

- **Standardizes practices** : Ensures that all team members adopt a consistent approach aligned with the company's consultative sales practices.

– **Encourages continuous improvement** : Regular training helps keep staff up to date with best practices and emerging technologies.

FUNDAMENTAL ELEMENTS OF CONSULTATIVE SALES TRAINING

- **Consultative selling fundamentals** : Ensure the team deeply understands what consultative selling is, including how it differs from traditional selling and the benefits of this approach.

- **Key Skills Development** : Focus on essential skills like active listening, empathy, negotiation and problem solving. Use role-plays and simulations for practice.

- **Use of CRM and technological tools** : Train your team in the effective use of CRM tools and other technologies that support the consultative sales process.

- **Product/service training** : Ensure all team members have in-depth knowledge of the products or services offered so they can effectively communicate value to customers.

- **Relationship Management** : Teach techniques for building and maintaining long-term customer relationships, which are vital to success in consultative selling.

IMPLEMENTING AN EFFECTIVE TRAINING PROGRAM

- **Needs assessment** : Start with an assessment of the team's current skills and identify areas that need development.

- **Personalized training** : Tailor training to the specific needs of your team and the types of clients they serve.

- **Continuous feedback and evaluation** : Incorporate regular feedback sessions and performance reviews to monitor progress and make adjustments to the training program as needed.

- **Incentives for continuous learning** : Establish a rewards system to encourage active participation and application of learned skills.

- **Ongoing support** : Provide ongoing support and learning resources to help staff keep their skills sharp and adapt to market and industry changes.

Training your sales team to implement consultative selling is an investment that pays dividends in the form of better results, greater customer satisfaction and a more engaged and motivated team. With proper training, your team will be better equipped to transform sales interactions into lasting, fruitful consultative relationships.

Ready to take the next step? In the next chapter, we'll discuss how to adjust your consultative approach to different cultures and markets, ensuring your team can operate effectively in a global environment. Stay with us to expand your ability to serve a diverse clientele.

CULTURAL ADAPTATION

Consultative selling, while focusing heavily on building relationships and customizing solutions, must be sensitive to cultural variations to be effective globally. This chapter explores how to adapt your consultative sales strategies to meet the cultural specificities of different markets, ensuring effective communication and successful business relationships.

THE IMPORTANCE OF CULTURAL SENSITIVITY IN CONSULTATIVE SALES

Cultural sensitivity is crucial because:

- **Improves communication** : Understanding cultural nuances can help you avoid misunderstandings and communicate your message more effectively.

- **Strengthens relationships** : Showing respect and consideration for cultural differences can strengthen mutual trust and respect between you and your international customers.

- **Increases sales effectiveness** : Adapting your approach according to the customer's cultural expectations can significantly increase the chances of sales success.

STRATEGIES TO ADAPT CONSULTATIVE SELLING TO DIFFERENT CULTURES

- **Research and education** : Before entering a new market, invest time in learning about the local culture, business practices, and communication preferences. This may include formal study, consultations with cultural experts, or direct immersion in the market.

- **Personalization of communication** : Adapt your communication style and methods to align with market cultural norms. For example, in some cultures, business relationships begin with extensive non-business conversation to build trust.

- **Adjust negotiation strategies** : Understand and respect local negotiation conventions, which can vary significantly. In some cultures, for example, directly discussing price can be seen as rude or insensitive.

- **Cultural team training** : Train your sales team in the cultural specificities of the markets in which they operate, ensuring that everyone is prepared to interact respectfully and effectively with customers from different cultural backgrounds.

- **Ongoing feedback and adjustments** : Maintain open lines of communication with customers and local partners to get regular feedback on how your approach is perceived and what adjustments may be needed to improve effectiveness.

PRACTICAL EXAMPLE

Suppose your software company is expanding into Japan, a market that highly values formality and long-term relationships. Adaptations can include using formal titles, preparing for longer, more detailed meetings, and taking a patient approach to building trust before discussing contractual details.

Adapting your consultative sales practices to account for cultural differences is essential to success in a globalized business environment. By developing a deep understanding of your international customers' cultural preferences and expectations, you can create more effective sales strategies and build lasting, respectful relationships.

In the next chapter, we'll explore ethics in consultative selling, emphasizing how maintaining high ethical standards can positively impact your business relationships and your company's reputation. Stay with us to learn how to integrate ethics deeply into your consultative sales strategies.

ETHICS AND CONSULTATIVE SALES

In consultative selling, ethics are crucial not only to building and maintaining customer trust, but also to sustaining a positive and lasting reputation in the market. This chapter discusses the importance of maintaining high ethical standards in consultative selling and offers guidelines for ensuring that your business practices respect and promote integrity in all interactions.

THE IMPORTANCE OF ETHICS IN CONSULTATIVE SALES

Ethics in consultative sales positively impacts:

- **Customer trust** : An ethical approach builds a solid foundation of trust, essential for long-term business relationships.

- **Business sustainability** : Ethical practices ensure that the business can operate without facing legal or reputational problems, which could compromise its sustainability.

- **Corporate culture** : A commitment to ethics strengthens corporate culture, attracting and retaining talent who value integrity and transparency.

RECOMMENDED PRACTICES FOR MAINTAINING ETHICS IN CONSULTATIVE SALES

- **Full transparency** : Always be clear and honest about the capabilities and limitations of your products or services. Avoid exaggerating benefits or hiding information that could influence the customer's decision.

- **Respect for customer privacy** : Treat all customer information with the utmost care and confidentiality. Follow all applicable data protection laws and regulations.

- **Fairness in negotiations** : Ensure that all negotiations are conducted fairly and that both sides feel respected and valued.

- **Social responsibility** : Consider the social and

environmental impact of your sales and business. Look for ways to minimize negative impacts and promote positive benefits for society and the environment.

- **Conflict resolution** : Develop effective mechanisms to resolve any disputes or disagreements that arise in a fair and equitable manner.

STRATEGIES FOR INTEGRATING ETHICS INTO DAILY OPERATIONS

- **Ongoing training and education** : Provide regular ethics training for the entire team, highlighting real cases and hypothetical scenarios for discussion.

- **Creating a code of conduct** : Develop and implement a code of conduct that clearly defines ethical expectations for everyone involved in sales and customer management.

- **Open communication channels** : Establish channels where employees can report ethical concerns anonymously and securely.

- **Monitoring and evaluation** : Regularly monitor sales practices and evaluate adherence to ethical standards. Use the insights to continually improve policies and procedures.

Maintaining high ethical standards is essential to the success and integrity of consultative selling. By adopting rigorous ethical practices, you not only protect your company from legal and reputational risks, but you also foster an environment where truly valuable business relationships can flourish.

Ready to explore consultative sales expansion strategies? In the next chapter, we'll discuss how to expand your consultative sales as your business grows, ensuring you can scale sustainably and effectively. Stay with us to learn more about the growth and expansion in consultative sales.

EXPANSION AND GROWTH

As your consultative sales business matures, expanding strategically becomes essential to sustaining growth and maximizing market potential. This chapter explores several effective strategies for scaling your consultative sales operations, ensuring that growth is sustainable and aligned with your business's core values.

IMPORTANCE OF STRATEGIC EXPANSION

Well-planned expansion can:

- **Increase customer base** : Reaching new markets and customer segments can significantly increase your revenues.

- **Diversify risks** : Expanding your service or product offering can help mitigate risks associated with dependence on a single market or type of customer.

- **Foster innovation** : Entering new markets can inspire innovation and improvements in your products or services.

EXPANSION STRATEGIES FOR CONSULTATIVE SALES

- **Development of new products/services** : Identify opportunities to develop new products or services that complement your current offerings, based on customer needs and feedback.

- **Exploration of new geographic markets** : Evaluate the feasibility of entering new geographic markets where your products or services can solve unique problems or fill market gaps.

- **Partnerships and strategic alliances : Form partnerships with other companies that can offer** complementary distribution channels or customer bases . This can accelerate your access to new markets with less initial investment.

- **Increased sales force** : Expand your sales team to support increased volume of operations and to enter new territories. Hiring local salespeople can be particularly effective when entering international markets.

- **Automation and scalability** : Invest in technologies that automate sales and customer management processes, allowing your team to handle a greater volume of business without compromising the quality of service.

CONSIDERATIONS WHEN PLANNING EXPANSION

- **Financial sustainability** : Make sure that expansion does not compromise the company's financial health. Carefully plan the costs involved and consider financing strategies if necessary.

- **Corporate culture** : As you grow, maintain the corporate culture that supports consultative selling. This includes ongoing training and effective communication of the values and practices that define your business.

- **Quality control** : Implement rigorous quality control processes to ensure that expansion does not dilute the quality of your service or product.

Expanding your consultative sales operations requires a meticulous and strategic approach. By carefully considering how and where to grow, you can ensure that your expansion not only increases your profits, but also strengthens your brand and customer relationships.

Ready to look into the future of consultative selling? In the next chapter, we'll explore future trends and the ongoing evolution of consultative selling, helping you prepare for market changes and stay competitive. Stay with us to discover how to stay ahead in the field of consultative sales.

THE FUTURE OF CONSULTATIVE SALES

As we move forward, the world of sales continues to evolve rapidly, influenced by new technologies, changing consumer behaviors and changing market dynamics. This final chapter offers insight into future trends in consultative selling and how you can prepare for these changes, ensuring your approach remains relevant and effective.

EMERGING TRENDS IN CONSULTATIVE SALES

- **Artificial intelligence and machine learning** : These technologies are becoming increasingly crucial for analyzing large volumes of customer data and personalizing the sales experience, offering accurate recommendations and predictive insights.

- **Remote and virtual sales** : Driven by the global pandemic, remote sales will continue to expand. This requires adjustments to the way relationships are built and maintained, with an increasing focus on the effectiveness of digital communication.

- **Sustainability and Corporate Social Responsibility (CSR)** : Consumers and companies are increasingly favoring partners who demonstrate social and environmental responsibility, influencing sales practices and product/service offerings.

- **Focus on customer experience** : Customer experience is at the heart of consultative selling and will continue to be a key area of differentiation and innovation, with companies seeking to offer increasingly integrated and user-centric solutions.

PREPARING FOR THE FUTURE

- **Investment in ongoing education and training** : Ensure that your team is always learning and adapting to new sales tools and techniques. Continuing education is essential to staying competitive.

- **Adoption of advanced technologies** : Stay up to date with the latest technologies and consider how they can be integrated into your sales strategy to improve efficiency and personalization.

- **Flexibility and adaptation** : Be prepared to quickly change your strategies and operations in response to changes in the market and consumer behavior.

- **Active listening and feedback** : Continue to practice active listening and request feedback regularly to understand your customers' evolving needs.

Consultative selling is not just a methodology, but a philosophy that puts creating genuine customer value above all else. By staying true to this philosophy, while adapting your practices to emerging trends, you can ensure that your sales approach continues to be effective and relevant, no matter what changes the future may bring.

This book offered a comprehensive guide to transforming your sales techniques from simple transactions to lasting strategic partnerships. We hope the strategies and knowledge shared here inspire you to continue your journey of growth and success in consultative selling. Thank you for accompanying us on this enriching journey.

As we turn the final page of this journey together, I sincerely hope that the learnings shared here have touched your heart and sparked new perspectives. If this book has brought you any value, I kindly ask that you take a few moments to leave a review on Amazon. Your words not only help me grow and hone my craft, but they also guide other readers in their quests for knowledge and inspiration. Your opinion is a valuable gift, both for me and for the community of readers looking for stories that transform. I sincerely thank you for sharing this journey with me and I hope we can meet again in the pages of a new adventure.

REGINALDO OSNILDO

Hello, I'm Reginaldo Osnildo, author and innovator in the areas of sales, technology, and communication strategies. My experience ranges from the academic environment, as a professor and researcher at the University of Southern Santa Catarina, to practice as a strategist at Grupo Catarinense de Rádios. With a PhD in sales narratives and digital convergence, and a master's degree in storytelling and social imaginary, I bring my readers a unique fusion of theory and practice. My goal is to provide knowledge in a simple, practical and didactic language, encouraging direct application in personal and professional life.

Yours sincerely

Reginaldo Osnildo

+55 48 991913865

reginaldoosnildo@gmail.com

www.ingramcontent.com/pod-product-compliance
Lightning Source LLC
Chambersburg PA
CBHW071949210526
45479CB00003B/861